BORN AMISH

by Barbara Yoder Hall

Published By
JACBAR PUBLICATIONS
Randolph, Ohio

ISBN 0-9606154-0-7

SECOND PRINTING

Published By
JACBAR PUBLICATIONS
Box 103 - Randolph, Ohio 44265

Printed in U.S.A.

Contents

Illustrated by

PATTY RAE SWEITZER

The strict old order Amish do not allow photographs to be taken of them, as they believe that pictures are a graven image.

The photograph on the cover is of the author's niece, Ranita Hochstetler. Ranita is not Amish but is wearing clothes belonging to the author.

PREFACE

The Amish are a people who are observed with admiration and a bit of envy by those outside their religion. We wonder how they are able to live so frugally and quietly in the midst of this costly and hectic society.

Just who are the Amish? They are a religious group and yet they are more than a religion. Tradition is really the key to their survival and existence today. Tradition, coupled with deep-rooted religious beliefs, is the reason there are more than 50,000 Amish people scattered throughout the United States and Canada. Pennsylvania, Ohio and Indiana used to be the home for 80% of these 'plain people', and although these three states are still where the majority live, they have begun colonies in nearly half of the 50 states. Some states are more conducive to their way of living than others. Since farming is their main way of life, their region needs to be productive soil country.

As farming land has become extremely scarce in recent years, the Amish menfolk have been forced into other areas of work to support their large families. Their main talent, other than farming, is carpentry. Anyone that has ever owned a desk, a grandfather clock, or a cupboard made by an Amish carpenter, will gladly attest to the fact that their craftsmanship is the best. Their work is always superior to anything sold commercially.

Although customs and practices among the Amish vary from district to district, according to the dictates of the local ministers, the Amish all have some common denominators. The first is their means of transportation . . . the horse and buggy. Although they will ride in cars, owned by non-Amish and even hire drivers to take them to doctors, etc., they believe that owning a car is a direct connection to the outside world that will eventually lead to their own demise.

Not only is horse-power their means of transportation, it is also their power for farming. Although there are some modern Amish who own tractors, most do not.

Another practice they have in common is the absence of electricity in the homes and barns. They believe this to be a modern convenience that leads to needless gadgets. They are permitted to use electricity in a home if perhaps they are farming for a non-Amish person and living in his house. If they would then buy that farm, they are required to have all electric wires removed from the house and grounds. Many Amish today have found a source of power that is permitted by their bishops. They have gasoline powered engines for their washing machines and tools for their carpentry trade. Yet, there are still many who abstain from even this convenience.

Probably the most obvious custom they all have is their very simple, yet unique, form of dress. The STRICTEST Amish womenfolk wear dark-colored, plain dresses with white organdy aprons and capes for Sunday. The dresses are long and cumbersome, extremely modest. They use no patterns such as the world knows. Instead, each dress is made exactly like the few others they own. In this area especially, they believe that to deviate from tradition is a great sin. On their head always is a covering, called a *"kop"*. The *"kop"* they wear on Sunday is made of white organdy and is pleated with tiny, meticulous, intricate pleats. For everyday they wear a black covering.

The menfolk wear plain blue shirts, all homemade by the women. The trousers, also homemade, are the broad-fall type, such as the old sailor pants. A straw hat for everyday and black hat for Sunday completes their wardrobe.

All wear very plain black shoes and stockings.

Jacob Amman, the founder of the Amish, believed very

strongly that in their plain dress they could best fulfill the scripture that teaches that one be separate from the world.

Another issue that the Amish feel strongly about is their church service. They do not have church houses. They believe owning a building to hold their services is a waste of money. They meet in their homes for their worship services. Each family that is able, takes their turn having *"Gma"*. These services are held every other Sunday and last between 3 and 4 hours. The singing and preaching is all in German.

The language, spoken in the home of the Amish, is Pennsylvania Dutch, which is a dialect of German and not a written language.

All of these customs are vital to their survival. As soon as a family adopts any conveniences (car, electricity, church building) they are no longer considered Amish. They are generally referred to as Mennonites. The Mennonites are also a religious sect, but they are less restrictive in their rules and dress. They were founded more than a hundred years before the Amish and vary as much as the Amish in their regulations.

THE CUSTOMS IN THIS BOOK ARE FROM THE STRICTEST FORM OF AMISH IN EXISTENCE.

MY FRIEND NAOMI

When there was snow on the INSIDE of the windowsill, you could be certain that the room was extremely cold. There was no heat at all in the upstairs bedroom where we ten Yoder children slept, but I didn't mind once I was snuggled deep inside the comforts. The only problem was getting up in the morning. We stayed in bed as long as we possibly could, but never went past the third call from Mother.

Amish houses are not ruled by clocks. There was the big one on the mantel and a small clock in the kitchen. We did not pay attention to either one of these. Our alarm clock was our mother.

"Harvey, Barbara, Ferdinand, Annie, get up *schnell!*" (quick). When Mom put that "*schnell*" on the end, we knew it was time. I could count to five, jump out from under the warm covers, quickly put on my dress . . . can't let my brothers see me in my *unaruck* (slip) . . . and get to the stove in the living room as fast as possible. By the time I got there, five or six brothers and sisters were usually claiming that valuable space around our only heating unit.

"Barbara, you feed the chickens this morning", Mom would say to me before I was

fully awake. I don't think I ever told Mom how much I hated chickens. Oh, well, if I fed them in the morning, then my sister Annie would have to gather the eggs in the evening and that was the one job I REALLY hated.

Annie would always say, "Barbara, this is how to do it. You reach in quickly and grab the chicken before she has a chance to peck you. If you do it slowly or start to hesitate, she'll go for your hand. Chickens know when you're afraid of them."

No matter how many times she would tell me that, I still could not do it as she did. Why, she even took the eggs right out from under the chickens without bothering to get the hen out of her nest. Now, that was brave!

I knew I'd better get moving or I'd be late leaving for school. My friend Naomi always waited for me at the fence, but I could tell when I kept her waiting too long. It wasn't anything she said; it was the tone of her voice . . . sort of long-suffering and patient. In fact, I often wondered why we were such good friends since we were so different. She wasn't afraid of chickens at all as I was.

We may have been different in temperament, but in looks we were very much alike. We both were a bit chunky due to all the *rivvel soup* we ate. Our dark dresses had to reach to the top of our shoes and our aprons were a few inches shorter than our dresses. Of course, we both had to cover our braided hair with a *kop* (covering). Naomi's hair was just a shade lighter brown than mine was and she seemed proud of the fact that her hair was curly. The natural curl made it difficult for her to keep all her hair tucked under her covering. Although sometimes I was sure she wasn't trying very hard to keep it under control.

Besides being a bit vain, she also bragged anytime she could. She told me the other day, before school, that they were getting 250 eggs a day. Although I didn't want the job of gathering more eggs, it still irritated me that Naomi's family always did things bigger and better than we did.

Growing up in a strict Amish home, she was taught the same as I, that a person does not boast, but I always could sense just a hint of pride in her voice when she talked about THEIR animals or THEIR gardens. Like the time Naomi met me at the fence on the way to school with a silly grin on her face. I knew right away she had something to tell me. She barely let me get my whole body through the fence before she blurted out, "Bossie had twins last night!"

I thought to myself, 'Wouldn't you know it, twin calves only happen once in about fifty births and THEY had to have a set. Our cows never had twins and probably never would. They're so dumb.'

I didn't tell her what I was thinking. I just told her that our cows would probably have twins, too.

She blabbed all day about her silly calves, totally ignoring me, her best friend. She did get put in her place at noon when we were eating our dinner. Smart-mouth Jakie Hershberger said to Naomi, "Were you in the barn when they were born?" She turned pink and hung her head. That question didn't need answering. We all knew she wouldn't have been allowed to watch a birth.

I probably wouldn't have been so upset about the calves if it wouldn't have happened right after THEY got the first roastin' ears from their garden. I reminded her then that OUR family ate the first peas in the spring.

All my silly jealousies were almost forgotten on this cold, snowy morning, as I was trying to get those dumb chickens fedand still have time to stand by the warm fire in the living room for awhile before we left for school. I guess I took too long because the older ones were coming in from the barn just then and it was time for breakfast.

"The field is snowed over, so you'll have to go out the lane this morning", our mother told us during breakfast. We bundled up against the bitter cold and trudged out the long lane where Naomi was waiting for me. I still had quite a distance to go, when I saw the look on Naomi's face. I knew immediately that she was delirious about something. Oh, great, I thought. They probably beat the odds and had another set of twin calves.

"Mein hen un buply", (We have a baby) she

blurted out before I even got to her. I told her I thought that was nice in about the same way I had told her I was glad about the calves.

We were only a few feet down the road when I discovered that I had forgotten my lunch. When I told Naomi that I had to go back for it, she said, "I have plenty. I would love to share it with you."

She said it so nicely that I almost forgot to be jealous of her. Being a good Amish family, we had babies all the time, too, but it so happened that we hadn't had a baby for over a year. I really did feel ashamed that I was jealous of her, but I couldn't help myself, especially when she started to walk ahead of me at the top of the hill to where a third-grader, Ella, was waiting for us. Naomi and I were fourth-graders and we didn't usually walk with the younger children.

I heard her tell Ella, *"S'buply is so schnuck."* (The baby is so cute.) That's all I heard all the way down the hill as others joined us in our walk. *"Schnuck, schnuck, schnuck."*

When we got to school, it started all over again. The scholars that came from other directions hadn't heard about it yet and neither had Mrs. Leiner, our teacher. You would have thought no one else ever had a *schnuck buply* before. Mrs. Leiner didn't even call the roll first, as she usually did. She said, "Has everybody heard that Naomi has a new baby sister?"

I mumbled something under my breath and

Mrs. Leiner asked, "Haven't you heard yet, Barbara?" I nodded my head, but I really wanted to stick out my tongue at someone, anyone. There are two nasty little things that the Amish children do. Since they are not boisterous people, they pinch each other and stick out their tongues . . . all behind their mothers' backs, of course.

I did manage to get through the morning, although I couldn't concentrate very well, watching her silly grin out of the corner of my eye. At noon, I automatically went to the furnace where we always put our lunch buckets to keep our egg sandwiches warm. I reached up on top of the shelf and it dawned on me, I'd forgotten my lunch. I sat back down at my seat, dejected, knowing Naomi would forget that she had agreed to share her lunch. Oh, well, I thought, someone will notice when I pass out this afternoon and I'll have to tell them it's because I didn't have any lunch.

Mrs. Leiner came to my desk and asked, "Why, Barbara, aren't you hungry?" I was ready to play on her sympathy when Naomi came up the aisle with her lunch. She stopped at my desk and took out of her lunch bucket . . . an apple, a *Schnitz* (dried apple) pie and half of a liverwurst and apple butter sandwich. After she laid them on my desk, she said to Mrs. Leiner, "Barbara forgot her lunch today and I have more than I need. Besides, I'm so excited today, I just can't eat."

Wow, the look on Mrs. Leiner's face was enough to make anyone sick. I knew she was thinking, "Isn't Naomi wonderful!" I didn't get too upset though, because she did give me my favorite sandwich — liverwurst and applebutter. And, regardless of how many *schnitz pies* I ate, I still loved them.

I don't know how I ever made it through that day, but finally it was time to go home and I was anxious to see if Naomi remembered that we used to walk together. We did, but it wasn't the same. A big gang walked with us.

"You'd think everyone's heard enough about the baby", I whispered to my sister Annie on the way home. I'm sure Annie sensed that I was jealous, but she never said so. She wasn't that kind of sister.

When we were ready to turn in our lane, Naomi, who still had another half mile to walk said to me, "Barbara, Mom said that I could have someone over to see the baby in about a week and, when I can, you'll be the first one I'll invite."

I couldn't believe my ears. What a friend!

As days passed, Naomi talked less about the baby, and things returned almost to normal. Once in a while, I would get a twinge of jealousy when she talked of holding her sister.

One morning, two weeks after the baby was born, we got to the end of the lane and Naomi wasn't there. I sat down on the milk can stand to wait for her. She was hardly ever late.

My big-mouthed brother Ferdinand said, "I bet Naomi decided to get herself a new friend.

I bet she even went to school without you."

"She sure didn't. You just get outta here!" I yelled back.

I waited as long as I dared; but finally I decided I'd have to go on or be tardy. I had memorized exactly what I was going to say to her, expecting that she'd be at school when I got there. I was going to tell her that I enjoyed our friendship, but from now on, Jemima and I would be run-around friends.

There were no Hershberger children at school when I got there and I was puzzled. I should have known that the only thing that ever kept an entire family out of school was death.

It was about mid-morning when a buggy pulled up. It was the man from the farm halfway between ours and Naomi's. He came to tell us that the baby had died.

After Mrs. Leiner and all of us girls cried for a while, I looked up and happened to catch my sister's eye. She smiled just a little as if to say, "I understand."

I hated to walk home that night. If only the snow wouldn't have been on the ground, then I could have kicked a can or a large stone all the way home. That's what I usually did when something was on my mind. Instead, I walked as fast as I possibly could and, for the first time, got home before anyone else. I could see in Mom's eyes that she already knew.

"Did you know that the Hershberger baby is in *Himmel*?" (Heaven) she asked. Without waiting for an answer she finished, "All babies are."

She couldn't have uttered more comforting words.

BROWN'S SCHOOL

I walked two miles to school and two and a half back. I realize that sounds impossible, but there really is a logical explanation.

As an Amish child, I had my share of chores to do in the morning before school, so in order to save time, my brothers and sisters and I would cut across the field on our way TO school. In the evenings, we weren't in a big hurry to get home to our chores, so we stayed on the road and came in the long lane . . . hence, it was two miles TO school and two and a half miles BACK.

"Come on . . . hurry, Barbara," my friend Naomi would holler across the field. "We're going to be tardy for school!" She'd wait for me at the fence and, being a true friend, she'd even hold the barbed wire apart for me to climb through. I was always careful not to tear my dress since I had only three or four in my entire wardrobe. Amish children seldom have more.

"What did you have for supper last night?" Naomi would ask, as we'd start down the road towards our one-room school house.

"Rivvel soup," I'd tell her and often she'd reply, "Me too."

We both ate a lot of soup. *Rivvel* soup had a

milk base, and we would drop into the boiling milk a crumb mixture of egg and flour. I don't know how nourishing it was, but it was filling and economical.

After we had walked a while in silence, she'd ask, "What do you have in your bucket?"

"Egg sandwich, again," I'd mumble. Most of the time, she'd say, "Me too." We ate a lot of egg sandwiches, too.

Naomi and I could hear the school bell ringing when we got to the top of the hill. We knew we'd have to walk a little faster or the teacher would mark us tardy. Our brothers and sisters were almost to the bottom of the hill already. It was hard to talk and walk fast at the same time.

Rather enviously, we speculated about who was ringing the bell this morning. This job belonged to the ones who arrived at school early; it seldom was Naomi or me. The bell had a long rope and whoever was ringing it had to grab hold of the rope, using the whole weight of the body to get it going.

About the bellringers, Naomi said, "They probably don't have as many chores to do as you and I. That's why they can get there early." I agreed. In fact, we agreed that they were probably lazy children and everyone knows that laziness is a sin.

The early birds had another job, and this one wasn't as pleasant as ringing the bell. They had to bring in the coal from the coalhouse and start the fire in the stove that stood in the corner of the schoolhouse. Now, this job, NEITHER of us minded missing! We did enough of that at home!

"Good morning, girls," Mrs. Leiner said as we slid into our seats. She was calling the roll just then. We had made it on time again, but barely.

The days were all pretty much the same, but oh, the welcome sound of Mrs. Leiner saying, "Will the fourth grade scholars please open their readers?"! This was my favorite time of the day, although I had to be careful not to show my enthusiasm too much. Not only would my classmates notice but, worse yet, my brothers and sisters might tell my mother that Barbara had an unusual interest in books. Since there were no books at home, this was my only contact with English words. The Amish believe that too much booklearning leads to worldly ideas.

There were eight grades in Brown's School and Mrs. Leiner taught all of them. The year I was in the fourth grade, there were no fifth graders. If there was only one pupil for a certain grade, Mrs. Leiner either promoted or demoted him or her according to her judgment. All the classes had from two to eight scholars.

That year was also the year that Atlee Schrock went up to the teacher's desk one day and showed her the lump under his arm. That was Atlee's last day in school. A few weeks later, his parents pulled up in their buggy, cleaned out his desk and whispered something to the teacher. After they left, Mrs. Leiner turned to the class and, while wiping her eyes, said so softly that we had to strain to hear, "Atlee is a very sick boy and will not come back to school." He died a few months later, and school was dismissed so everyone could go to the funeral.

Besides not ringing the bell, there was something else Naomi and I never got to do. That was to sit on the same seat and study together. My brother Danny always sat with his friend Mahlon to study. Not only that, they were allowed to sit at the last desk in the back of the school. Now, to be able to sit in the last seat and be allowed to study with a friend, you had to be a very quiet and obedient student. I only remember sitting in the back one year and I don't remember ever studying with a friend. Of course, I would have studied with Naomi.

I told myself I didn't really need to study with anyone since I was an "A" student. Because I got such good grades, everyone used to call me "teacher's pet." Everyone but Naomi, that is. I didn't argue with them about it, because then I would have had to admit that I loved the books and what was in them. You could tell the teacher was pleased with me. Can you imagine teaching a group of passive Amish children for years and never igniting even a spark for learning more than was absolutely necessary?

After a day just like the one before had been . . . . reading, writing, arithmetic, recess, Andy-Over, egg sandwiches and spelling, the final bell for the day would ring. Often, Naomi and I would walk far behind the rest of the scholars because we would discuss the day's events, such as who wore a new dress, whose family had just had a new baby, who got in trouble with Mrs. Leiner for whispering too loudly, etc.

When we lagged too far behind the others, Naomi would say, "Let's catch up with the rest, 'cause a car might go by."

I didn't argue because I didn't like cars either. We were both taught that bad people rode around in cars. Although these were buggy roads, a car would occasionally pass through our Amish district. When it did, we would often hide in the ditch until it passed.

Once, while we were hiding, Naomi whispered to me, "I heard that people in cars sometimes shoot you."

Naomi wouldn't lie to me. We were friends.

Brown's School still stands on the crossroads about four miles north of Fredericksburg, Ohio. There's no name on the door. It doesn't need one. Everyone that needs to, knows it's Brown's School.

Every so often, I visit the school to keep my memories alive. One summer, I took my four sons to see it and they giggled as they walked around it. The yard had grown up like a

hayfield, and I was disturbed by it. I'm sure the boys were thinking, "No wonder Mother isn't any smarter, having to get her education here."

They kept asking me if I was sure that they still held school in this building. Just then a buggy passed by and I asked the young lady (in Pennsylvania Dutch to impress my sons) if school was still being held here. She said that it was.

I asked Mother later about the grass being all grown up and why it hadn't been mown down. She said, a little astonished that I had to ask, "But Barbara, why would they have to mow it when there is no school during the summer?"

I did drive past Naomi's house that day and saw her mother sitting on the porch. I would have liked to stop and ask how many children Naomi had now, but I didn't. The boys were restless and bored with their journey into their mother's past.

THE DOLL

Summer days often began in the strawberry patch or in the garden, depending on what was ripe. We Yoder children knew to start early in the morning picking what was ready to be canned that day. That way we could be out of the hot sun by noon. But our work was far from over even then. We still had to help wash jars, clean the fruit or vegetable and complete all other tasks that go with cold-packing food for winter.

An Amish child learns very young to work hard since they're taught that idleness is a sin.

I really didn't mind picking strawberries nearly as much as some of the picking we had to do. Green beans, for instance. There's just no fun in harvesting anything you can't eat as you go. And whoever heard of eating raw green beans? Now raw peas . . . that's a different story. (They ARE edible, honest!) But strawberries are the very best fruit or vegetable to eat right out of the garden, dirt and all. Of course, everyone knows there are some strawberries that simply can't be put into the basket. Maybe about a half a quart can get filled, then you find yourself holding one in your hand that just has to be eaten . . . it's THAT perfect.

Near noon, we'd join Grandma, Mother, and some of the older sisters in the kitchen that was already filled with the smell of strawberries being cold-packed. We knew we had a long day ahead of us. Mother always knew just how much to plant so that we'd have at least 200 quarts of everything. Of some vegetables, like the beans, we'd have closer to 300 quarts.

"Dinner is on," Mom said, when we came in from the strawberry patch. The Amish always call lunch "dinner." That day, dinner was strawberry soup, which simply means sugared strawberries drenched with milk and bread broken into it. We knew we'd have the same thing for supper that night. Whatever we were canning was alway served for the meals on that day . . . nothing else. A person can fill up on roastin' ears if they're really hungry . . . or green beans or peas.

About mid-afternoon, Mother would say, "If some of you want to go after the mail now, you can go." We never needed a second invitation. All of us "Middle" children would go. Not that it took that many to bring in the mail; it was just one of the few breaks we would get in a summer's day of work.

An Amish mailbox usually holds very little. In fact, I could just about tell what would be in the box before I opened it. "The Ohio Farmer," a periodical for farmers, came once a month and I loved it because it had one cartoon in it which we were not supposed to read. I always read it anyway coming down the lane before Mother had a chance to tell me not to look at it.

Another item in every Amish mailbox is "The Budget", published in Sugarcreek, Ohio. This paper is devoured by the Amish, especially my grandmother, who would go into her room after it arrived and not come out for days, except to eat. These papers were like letters from friends. There is a writer in all Amish communities that tells "The Budget" of all that's going on. Their favorite subject is who had what kind of illness and they don't spare the details. It is not at all unusual to read of someone vomiting quite a bit. Of course, births, deaths, weddings and visiting one another are favorite subjects. Even animal births and deaths are written about.

Except for an occasional letter from *freundshaft* (kinfolk), the only other mail was the milk check and a bill from the local doctor for some of the last Yoder babies that he had arrived in time to deliver. We did get the *Sears & Roebuck* catalogue, which we used in many ways.

As we got near the end of the lane on this particular summer day, we could tell the mailbox held more than usual because the lid didn't close all the way. We all took off running, trying to be the first to see what the package was.

Brother Ferdinand said, "It's probably my boots that Mom ordered from the catalogue.

She told me I needed boots worse than the rest of you."

He always knew just what to say to make all of us mad, but we didn't argue with him. He was bigger than any of us. But he got what he deserved that day. The package was address to Barbara Yoder. That was me, and I could not believe my eyes. Surely there must be some mistake. An Amish child does not receive mail, much less a package. The return address said "Ada Hess" who was a distant cousin who was not Amish and had come to visit recently from Indiana. Why she had singled me out of the seven Yoder girls to send a gift to is something I'll never know. But I was not going to argue with Fate. I ripped open the package with the undivided attention of my brothers and sisters, even Ferdinand.

I don't imagine anyone could describe the shock and amazement on our faces as we stared at "THE DOLL", lying in the shoe box. It was a hard plastic doll like one I had seen in the catalogue, but never in person.

The only doll I'd ever seen was my friend Naomi's Amish doll. Her mother had made it out of cloth and dressed it in Amish clothes so that it looked almost like Naomi herself. The only thing different was that Amish dolls do not have faces because it makes them look worldly. I'd always envied Naomi for having a real doll. All we ever had was blankets rolled up, which we pretended were doll babies.

Just wait till Naomi sees this, I thought to

myself. For once she'll be jealous of me! Everyone talking at once brought me back to reality.

"She's ugly," Brother Ferdinand teased.

"She sure isn't," three-year-old Lizzie piped up.

"Can I carry it awhile?" Annie asked.

The boys were interested for only a few minutes but then they took off, knowing that dolls were for girls. My sisters helped me carry it in the rest of the way. We didn't even speak much; we were so awed by this magnificent plaything.

I entered the kitchen carrying the only store-boughten toy I had ever owned, except for the sled that we all shared.

"Look what Cousin Ada sent me!" I said, showing my prize to my sisters, Mom and Grandma. If I hadn't been so wrapped up in my delight, I would have seen the looks on their faces, but I didn't. Dad wasn't home but there was one more person in the family who had not seen my beautiful doll.

"Vo ist de Dawdy?" (Where is Grandfather?) I asked my grandma. I took off for the basement, where she had said he was. I had gone only about halfway down the steps when I met him coming up. I thrust the doll right into his arms, blabbering excitedly, "Look what Cousin Ada sent me!"

His hair was white and so was his long

beard, but all that hair could not hide the lightning that came to his eyes at the sight of the doll. He never said one word, but with a deliberate aim crashed it to the cement where it broke into many, many pieces. It was a hard plastic and shattered immediately.

"A worldly doll you do not need!" he said, as he brushed on past me.

Annie and I were both crying as we stared at the heap of plastic. I held up the hem of my dress like I usually did to gather eggs, while Annie picked up the pieces and deposited them in my make-shift basket.

"Why did he do it?" I asked Annie between sobs as we dumped the pieces on the burn pile.

"Barbara, you know Mom wouldn't have let you keep the doll either. It is a worldly toy and it would have only made you want more things that you don't need. You know what they say, 'Today a doll, tomorrow a car.' Don't hate Grampa. You know he's a kind man."

We stayed outside for a long while that afternoon, and Mom didn't call out for us to get back to work. She knew we would as soon as we could. When we did walk back into the kitchen, there was a silence I had never heard before . . . almost like death. Annie and I picked up a bowl of strawberries and started cleaning them. I never knew that a clock could tick so loud.

After we had worked in silence for a long

while, Mom said, "Barbara, Grandma and I are going to make a doll for you."

Smiling through my tears, I asked her, "This one won't break, will it, Mom?"

ESTHER

Naomi and I didn't like Esther the minute we saw her. We were putting our lunch buckets on the shelf by the furnace when I caught an unusual color out of the corner of my eye.

I poked Naomi in the ribs and whispered, "Do you see what I see? She must be a relative of Mrs. Leiner's. She couldn't possibly be going to attend OUR school."

Mrs. Leiner was the teacher for our one-room, Amish school and sometimes she brought along a neice for just a day. Surely this girl in the loud pink dress must be a relative of hers.

In the Amish world, there is no pink — only dark colors, like brown, blue or black. Therefore, no one could blame we Amish children for staring at this strange-looking, worldly girl that stood in our midst this morning.

Mrs. Leiner tapped her pencil on her desk, which was the signal for us to take our seats.

"Good morning, scholars," she said after everyone was seated and quiet. "I'm sure you've noticed that we have a new scholar this morning." (She always called us "scholars" or "pupils.") She never called us "students" for that word was too modern.

"Oh, great," I thought. "She really is going to go to OUR school."

"The name of our new girl is Esther," Mrs. Leiner continued, interrupting my nasty thoughts.

"Esther, what a dumb name." I wasn't sure whether I said that out loud or not, but since no one said anything, I must not have.

"I want all of you to be nice to Esther and welcome her to our school," Mrs. Leiner continued.

I sure was glad she didn't give her a seat right in front of me. I couldn't have helped but yank those long pigtails hanging down her back. How worldly can you get? Everyone knows pigtails are supposed to be wrapped around your head and put under a covering.

We finally got to recess time, although I do admit, I couldn't concentrate with that terrible pink dress, so obnoxious, three seats in front of me. As soon as we were dismissed for recess, Naomi and I met behind the outhouse. Because of the smell, not too many children played around it. It was the one place we could go to be alone. Today we had a lot to discuss.

"Did you hear her name?" I asked Naomi. "Esther . . . what a dumb name."

"But Barbara, Esther is a Bible name," Naomi said.

"I know, but so is Jezebel," I told her. "And

besides, it's just typical Mennonite." We were taught that the Mennonites were the same as people of the world.

I was just starting to tell Naomi what I thought of Esther's pink dress and those pigtails hanging shamefully down her back, when Naomi grabbed my arm and jerked me behind the building.

"What'd you do that for?" I yelled at her. "You hurt my arm!"

"Didn't you see her? She had a picture-taking box," Naomi said.

I peeked around the corner and, sure enough, there she stood with a black square box up to her eye. I recognized it from the Sears and Roebuck catalogue.

Naomi and I were certain that Esther knew that the Amish were not permitted to have their pictures taken. It says so right in the Ten Commandments: "Thou shalt not make unto thee any graven images."

I was ready to march right up to her and really tell her off when the bell rang for us to go back to class. On the way in, I told Naomi that I would tell Mrs. Leiner what Esther was doing at recess.

She was already at her seat when I got to mine. I could tell that no one else was doing their duty and telling the teacher, so it would have to be me. I started up the aisle until I got right beside Esther's desk. I looked down at her with a look of "You've had it now, girl." I shouldn't have stopped. She looked up at me with a grin and when I looked at her hand, she had a piece of gum in it.

She cooed, "Would you like it?"

Wow! This was May and I hadn't had gum for many months. I did get a pack at Christmas, but it was all gone before February. Even when I made one stick of gum last a week by putting it on the bedpost at night, it seemed that my gum was always gone in no time.

"It's Juicy Fruit," Esther drooled, cracking her already soft and pliable gum. (Oooooh, my favorite!)

"Barbara, we're ready to start now," Mrs. Leiner said. I grabbed the gum and quickly sat down. I could hardly concentrate, smelling that Juicy Fruit gum. I was saving it until after lunch.

At noon, Naomi asked me if I had told Mrs. Leiner. I told her that I felt it our Christian duty to give Esther another chance to behave herself.

As soon as I had eaten my lunch, I got that piece of Juicy Fruit in my mouth and decided it was worth it.

We were getting ready to go home when Mrs. Leiner said, "Esther has something to tell the class."

Esther stood before the class with a big grin on her face and that stupid black box in her hand.

"Oh, great," I thought. "She's going to show us the pictures she took today."

"In order for me to take pictures, there has to be film in the camera, and I haven't had film in my camera all day," Esther said teasingly.

Naomi and I walked home slowly the day Esther pulled her camera trick. We had a lot to talk about. I waited until everyone was far ahead of us, then I told her my secret.

"I knew all along there was no film in the camera," I said. I could see the admiration in Naomi's eyes for her friend who was so wise to the world. When we got to the top of the hill, we were in for a surprise. There stood Esther, waiting for us.

"Do you like your gum, Barbara?" she asked.

"Yes," I said, "But do you have one for my friend, Naomi?"

She dug in her pocket and handed Naomi a piece of Spearmint gum. I couldn't believe it. She actually had two kinds of gum at the same time.

She walked with us until we got to her road, where she turned off. As we walked the rest of the way, we didn't talk much. We just chewed our gum, cracking it and blowing bubbles. When we got to my lane where I had to leave Naomi, I told her, "Naomi, Esther gets two packs of gum a week. Do you think she could be a run-around friend with us?" Naomi said that she thought too that we should be nice to Esther.

In the fall when we came back to school, Esther wasn't there. I sure was looking forward to some more Juicy Fruit gum. When Naomi and I asked Mrs. Leiner about Esther, she told us that her family decided to send her to Fredericksburg to the public school. Naomi and I felt kind of bad about that.

THE WEDDING

Amish weddings are the most important social events of the year, especially for the young people. Since there is so little opportunity to play the mating-dating game, weddings offer the very best time to match up.

After receiving an invitation verbally from the bride and groom about a week before the wedding, an Amish family would never miss this occasion to get together and socialize. For days, they waited for that buggy to come in the lane and the soon-to-be-married couple to say, "You're invited to our wedding." Of course, they had been "published" (wedding date announced) the previous Sunday in the church service.

When Amanda Stolzfus got married to Abe Byler, I was ten years old and just the right age to dream that someday *I* would be in Amanda's shoes. The ultimate goal for any Amish young lady is to be married. To reach the age of twenty-one and have no future husband in sight is a sure sign that you are destined to be single for life. To never be a wife is sad enough, but never to bear children, even sadder.

But I knew *I* would be like Amanda. I'd have a steady, come-calling boyfriend at eighteen and by twenty or twenty-one, I'd ride from farm to farm with my intended, inviting people to MY wedding.

I could hardly wait for THE BIG DAY, Amanda and Abe's wedding. All Amish weddings are held in the coldest winter months. Abe and Amanda not only waited until the harvest was in, they even planned their wedding after the November butcherings. Being loyal Amish, they knew summer weddings were inconvenient because of the farm work and impractical because they had no refrigeration for the meat they would serve at the wedding feast. They could choose between two days of the week . . . Tuesday or Thursday. They picked Tuesday.

Tuesday morning finally arrived. It felt like Sunday to we ten Yoder children as we dressed in our good outfits for this important occasion. It had been several years since we'd been invited to a wedding and I hardly remembered anything about it. But this one was going to be different. I'd start observing a little more, now that I was older, for the time when *I* would be the lucky girl to say, "I do."

The winter snow in our lane was too deep for the buggy, so we hitched up the sleigh. I really didn't like riding in the sleigh . . . it was completely open and much colder than the buggy; but since I was so excited about going to the wedding, I think I would have even walked.

As I climbed into the sleigh, lifting my long dress just enough to get my foot up on the step, I thought again of my friend, Naomi. Poor Naomi. Her family hadn't received an invitation. Being a loyal friend, I didn't talk about the wedding too much at school after I found out they were not invited.

Naomi had told me at school on Monday, "Barbara, when you come back to school on Wednesday, I want you to tell me all about the wedding." She had left me specific instruction. I was to tell her who the *"hostler"* was, who the *"nava huckers"* were and which boys and girls sat together for the wedding feast. This pairing-off for the meal was often indication of weddings to come. But never would a young Amish fella ask a girl himself to sit with him. First time "dates" are always arranged by a go-between, a *hostler*. The *"nava huckers"* or attendants were usually couples who were already going steady.

As our sleigh neared the Troyer farm (neighbor's of the bride's) where the wedding service was going to be held, we could see buggies and sleighs coming from all directions. Amish weddings are always held at a near neighbor's house so that the home of the bride can be used to prepare and serve the meal. Amish weddings are often attended by at least 300. The Troyer farm had two houses, as do most Amish farms. There is the big house and the *"dawdy"* (grampa) house. By putting benches throughout both houses and in upstairs bedrooms as well, they would be able to seat everyone comfortably for the three or four hour service.

We had sung two songs when the preachers and the wedding party filed in quietly. They had been in another room of the house for the first half hour of the service in which the ministers had given marriage instructions to the bride and groom. Of course, the first thing I noticed was Amanda's new dress. It was made over the same pattern that all of our dresses were made from but this one had such a new look to it. Not at all the worn and washed look that all of our dresses had. Since our only permitted colors were black, dark brown and dark blue, Amanda picked dark blue. It appeared to my curious eyes that the shade of her dress was just a bit lighter than we were usually permitted to have.

I sat quietly beside my mother during the long service. Oh, how I yearned for the day when *I* could sit with the other girls and wear a grownup cape and apron. Mine was still a child's apron that had a small button in the back. Theirs had to be pinned with straight pins in the front as the cape criss-crossed across their breast to hold the bosom securely in place. No old-order Amish lady is permitted to wear a bra, which is considered figure revealing. With the heavy dresses and the specially designed capes, the Amish feel they are more modest than if they would wear a brassiere. As an observant eight-year-old I had heard gossiping rumors about young ladies that were discovered wearing those worldly uplifting contraptions.

My mind kept wandering to other rumors that I had heard in school, while the preacher droned on. I did enjoy the singing, but the sermons were so hard to understand. They were in German. We spoke Pennsylvania Dutch, which is a dialect of the German and is an unwritten language. Some of the words were the same in German and Dutch so that I understood enough to follow the service and know when they were getting to the good part. That was when the bride and groom would stand beside each other and "be joined as one."

When I really got bored, my mind turned to the food we would soon consume. All week, many neighbor women had baked pies, cookies and cakes for this important occasion. Chickens had been frying in skillets since early in the morning of the wedding. Soon we would be enjoying this feast of mashed potatoes, noodles, gravy, peas, corn, lima beans, red beets, pickles, chicken, meat loaf, *schnitz pies*, bread, cookies, many different kinds of pies and cakes.

During the meal, I peeked in the living room to see the bride and groom sitting in the corner. There is always a corner table where the couple can sit facing each other. Their attendants sit on either side of them. For hours, the food kept coming, as those who finished eating would get up and let other guests take their place at the tables. I ate in the kitchen with my mother that day. I would liked to have eaten in the living room so that I could watch the bride and groom open their gifts, but then I would have had to wait much longer to eat and by then I was starved.

I had watched intently as the *"hostler"* went from boy to girl doing his fixing up for the day. I knew it wouldn't be too many more years until I would be the one to blush as word came that some young man wanted to sit with me at the meal. I had memorized who all the couples were so that I could tell Naomi the next day in school about the matches.

After I finished my meal, I stood inside the living room door and watched the newly-weds as they lifted each gift above their heads and announced the name of the giver. There were many pots, pans, dish cloths and towels, sheets, oil lamps and all the other necessary items they would need to set up housekeeping.

When everyone was finished eating and all the gifts were opened, the singing began. These songs were much better than the ones I was accustomed to. The young people sang them at the Sunday evening singings, but since I was too young to attend those gatherings, weddings were the only time I heard those beautiful songs.

They weren't slow and mournful like the ones I was used to hearing in the church service. Their tempo was faster and some were even sung in English. I sure did like them.

Just as the good part was about to begin,

Dad said it was time to go home and Mom started to gather up the children. I really wanted to stay longer and see if it was true what Naomi had said about some of the couples going out to the barn late in the evening at weddings and dancing on the threshing floor of the barn. She said that some young fella always brought a harmonica and that some of the more worldly couples square danced. I couldn't believe it was true, but Naomi wouldn't lie to me.

As we piled into the sleigh for the ride home, I thought of the newly-weds and of what lay ahead of them. Tonight they would sleep at the bride's house where the wedding had been held and tomorrow they would help clean up the mess from the feast. Then, for several days, they would visit relatives before settling down and starting their housekeeping.

I snuggled down into a blanket to keep warm on the sleigh ride home, dreaming that someday *I* would be setting up housekeeping and caring for my own babies. I was sure it would be different from caring for my brothers and sisters. They were such a bother.

I fell asleep that night, contented and happy. It had been a good day. I just knew that somewhere God was preparing a young man to be my husband and, when that wonderful day of MY wedding did take place, there was no doubt in my mind that Naomi would be one of my attendants. That is, if *I* got married first, which I was sure I would.

Photographs

A WORD ABOUT THE AMISH AND PHOTOGRAPHS—

The Amish believe that having their pictures taken is wrong because it is a graven image. Therefore, during the author's first eleven years there are no photographs of her family.

This family picture was taken soon after they left the Amish church and although they were no longer Amish, the clothes still reflect their strict previous life.

Ferdinand, Cora, Mattie, Danny
Harvey, Lizzie, Fannie
Barbara, Mom (holding Mose, Jr.) Dad, Katie, Anna

Mom

Perhaps in some of these photgraphs you may see the transition from the Amish dress to the more liberal styles they wear today. You cannot see in these photographs the new colors that entered their life.

Mom and Dad

Cora, Mattie, Ferdinand
Lizzie, Harvey

The Four Brothers

Barbara holding Mose, Jr.

The Family Today

Cora, Martha, Ann, Barbara, Liz, Fran, Kathy

Ferd, Harvey, Mose, Dan

DAWDY

THE FUNERAL

The buggy wheels spit the gravel in all directions, grinding, grinding, grinding. My stare was fixed — almost hypnotized — watching the stones fly in all directions. The methodical turning of the wheels added to my trance-like condition. My spell was broken occasionally by the sniffles of my little grandma who was sitting beside me on the back buggy seat. My father and brothers were riding on the front seat. Amish menfolk always ride up front, characteristic of their position in life.

Although I would miss my Grandpa too, it couldn't begin to match my Grandma's grief. She'd look up for a minute at the coffin buggy directly ahead of us and watch the wooden box containing the body of her husband of forty-five years, jiggling around on the back of the specially-made Amish hearse. An Amish hearse is simply a one-seated open buggy with a long platform in back . . . just the right size to hold the standard six-sided wooden coffin. Occasionally the coffin buggy would hit a rut in the road and it seemed to me that the wooden box would actually fly off, but it didn't. That is when my Grandma's sniffles would become audible sobs and that made me cry too.

I was nine years old when Grandpa died and, although I had gone to funerals all my life, this one was different. This was my first flesh and blood.

"Is it much longer?" I whispered to my mother.

We'd traveled an hour already and I was getting a little restless. Besides, I had sat very quietly during the three and a half hour funeral service. Surely the cemetery couldn't be too much further.

"Not too much farther now," she whispered back. Since the Amish are not boisterous people, everything is said quietly, especially at funerals.

It was almost supper-time when we reached a little private graveyard owned by the Amish. The buggies left the road and crossed the field to the back corner, where Grandpa's grave was waiting for his body. The men from the church had opened the grave the day before the funeral.

As I stepped from the buggy, I couldn't believe how many buggies were coming up the field. I should have known by the size of the funeral that many would come to participate in this last ritual of the funeral process. Although Amish funerals are well attended, between 300 and 600, my grandfather's was exceptionally large since he was a well-known and respected man in the community. In fact, he gave *zeigness* in the church. After every church service, several religious patriarchs always gave *zeigness* (witness) that what they heard that day in the sermons was scriptural.

My sister Cora could see that I wasn't too anxious to go near the open grave, so she took me by the hand and said, "Come, I'll stay beside you."

After one last look at my grandfather's face, the men screwed the lid of the coffin shut forever. They lowered it into the fresh earth on straps and then started the task of covering the hole with the mounds of dirt. Four men positioned themselves at each corner of the hole and, at the sound of the mournful song of a small group of men, the grave singers, the shovels went into action. Four replacements stood by to take over the shoveling job when the first four tired. The eight then alternated until the job was done.

The sounds of that burial have stayed with me always . . . the songs, the sobbing and the shoveling.

Later a stone would be erected. It would say: Ferdinand F. Miller - 1861 to 1949.

It was almost dark when we finally got back to our farm and supper. The event that had interrupted our humdrum life three days ago was almost over . . . but not quite. The rest of the evening was spent in listing Grampa's good deeds and the facts of his wholesome life, repeating the same things that had been discussed since the moment he died. The main thought was always, "I'm sure he made it to Heaven."

The Amish believe that the only way to

attain eternal life is to despise the world and abstain from its pleasures and conveniences.

While the grownups visited, I wandered to the door where Grandpa had lain dead for three days. It was his bedroom when he was alive. I didn't go in. I was afraid. I could still picture him lying in his bed while the undertaker worked on him. I wasn't supposed to see that, but when a neighbor lady was washing the windows of that room the day he died, I climbed up the ladder behind her and, before I was discovered and shooed down, I saw a sight that haunted me until well into my teens.

For two years, Grandpa had lain in that bed, tended by his loving and devoted wife. Since we lived in the same house, we often helped our Grandma with her tasks of caring for him. Sometimes he would wander away, since his mind had slipped in later years, so we would take him by the hand and lead him back into the warm house. At times, he only wanted my sister Annie to lead him back. Finally, the time came that even Annie couldn't safely bring him home . . . he had hit her with his cane.

Oft times he would cry out in his bed for us to bring him out of the cornfield or wheatfield back into the house. The only thing that would reassure him that he was actually inside was we children singing. Grandma would say, "Come children, sing for *Dawdy* again." We only knew a few songs from the church service, but neither *Mummy* or *Dawdy* minded our repeating them over and over.

I was supposed to be sleeping the night he died, but being in the next room and hearing all the grownups talking softly, I knew it wouldn't be long. Sure enough, the next morning we awoke to the news that *Dawdy* was asleep forever. That's when all the action started. The family didn't have to do a thing but mourn. The coffin maker was notified, the undertaker called for and the neighbors came swarming in to get the house and barn ready for the funeral.

They scrubbed the house spotless, brought in food and prepared it. The men worked on the barn, especially the threshing floor where it was decided that the main service would be held. The overflow would sit in the house, preached to by a second set of preachers.

Even though I was upset by my grandfather's death, I nevertheless somewhat enjoyed those days of not having to be in the field, garden, barn or kitchen, working from sunup until sundown. The neighbors did ALL the work.

We lived in that house for two more years after Grandfather's passing and I never entered THAT room alone, even in the daylight. It always had the smell of death.

OUR DAY

I told my sister Annie, as we were cleaning out the big iron kettle, that I sure was glad we didn't have to have church at our house more than once a year.

The Amish hold their services in the homes of their members and, when our "turn" came, we knew we had lots of work to do. Not that our house was so dirty . . . it was just that, since the Amish judge each other's housekeeping abilities so severely, Mother demanded that everything be spotless and in order.

"Why on earth do we have to clean the wash house?" I asked my older and wiser sister that day.

"Well, maybe someone will bring their child out here to *bletch*, if he doesn't behave," Annie told me. "You know Jonas's little ones don't always sit very still in church."

I could picture a woman bringing her errant child out here, spanking him or her and then taking inventory so she could tell the other women later in the day about Mary Yoder's wash house.

I really felt sorry for Jonas's children. I had my share of *bletchings* too. It was hard, sitting quietly for over three hours and on those benches yet . . . so hard and no backs.

I always felt that the reason the Amish only have church every other Sunday was that you got enough preaching to last you two weeks. I'm sure that wasn't the reason, but I did have a habit of getting ideas a good Amish child wasn't supposed to have. I often wondered why I did that. I lived in the same sheltered environment my nine bothers and sisters lived in and they didn't seem to show my signs of inquisitiveness. It was probably that Sears and Roebuck catalogue. I loved it. After it served its first purpose — ordering galoshes — it made its way to the outhouse for its final uses. That is where I used to sit by the hour and look at the weird people and their clothes. I couldn't believe people actually went out in public looking like that. I always hated to tear out the pages with the pretty dresses to crinkle up and use, so I left them till last, using instead the pages with lawn mowers, garden tools and other such boring equipment.

"Barbara, you're daydreaming again." Annie reminded me for the third time. "Mom said she wanted this washhouse clean by dinner." Dinner is the noon meal for the Amish. The evening meal is supper.

"Do you think this kettle is clean enough for the soup?" I asked her.

I sure hoped so. My arms were aching from scrubbing. Besides, my bulky dress didn't make it easy to bend over the rim of the huge pot that would hold enough bean soup to feed over 200 people.

On Sunday morning, Mom would build the fire under the kettle before church and, after melting the butter and adding the cooked beans, we would pour in gallons and gallons of rich, unseparated milk.

I will admit there was one advantage of having church at our house. I got to stay out of the service and watch the kettle of milk so that it wouldn't boil over. Then, as soon as church was let out, around one o'clock, Mom and some of the women of the congregation would put in the dry bread chunks and dish it out into smaller kettles to be taken into the house for the people to eat.

We finally finished the wash house and Annie said that she thought it would pass Mom's inspection. As soon as we walked into the kitchen to eat, Mom said, "Barbara, after dinner, you and Harvey clean around the corn crib . . . real good."

"First the washhouse and now the corn crib." I muttered to Annie. "Who is going to look at THAT old building?"

She didn't even answer me. That's what she did when I asked dumb questions. It wasn't nearly as bad cleaning the corn crib as I had thought it was going to be since Harvey remembered to bring along a rubber ball so we could play Andy-Over when Mother wasn't watching.

We played "Andy Over" a lot at school, but there we had a big gang and that made the game more fun. We divided into two teams and threw a rubber ball over a building to each other. If someone caught the ball the whole gang would come around the side of the building and tap someone on the other side, thereby making them a part of that team. On this particular day we had to settle for the few brothers and sisters we could enlist.

When we came in for supper after chores, there stood Annie cleaning the oil lamps.

"That's not fair," I told her, "Mom never lets ME clean them. And it's not because I'm only eight . . . you were cleaning them when you were that young."

My brother Ferdinand heard me complain and, since he didn't care whether he made me mad or not, said, "Maybe Mom still remembers the one you dropped last summer. They don't come cheap, you know."

I stuck my tongue out at him. Amish children are known for sticking out their tongues and pinching each other.

I could hardly sleep Saturday night, just thinking of the BIG DAY. Mom got us up early Sunday morning . . . much earlier than usual. Chores were done as quickly as possible, breakfast eaten and dishes washed, and then it was time to set up the benches. Amish homes are sparsely furnished, so stacking the furniture in one small bedroom was an easy task. The benches were then placed very close to each other in all the rooms on the main floor . . . kitchen, living room, and big bedroom.

Each district owned its own set of benches which were carted on the bench wagon to each service.

If the first floor didn't hold the entire congregation, the overflow — usually the teenagers — sat in upstairs bedrooms.

"Girls, go and get dressed for church now," Mom said. She didn't have to tell us what to wear; we had only one or two Sunday dresses. The colors allowed in OUR congregation were dark brown, dark blue and black. These colors not only applied to our dresses, it also meant our curtains were to be one of the three.

We girls had all been freshly braided the day before, so the only attention our hair needed was a few *"struvvles"* brushed back. It did give us a chance to glance into THE mirror. We were only allowed one mirror in the house. It was very small, kept in a drawer and used only when absolutely necessary. Sometimes, Mom would catch us looking at ourselves a tad too long and we would get the vanity sermon.

After I put on my heavy dark brown dress that came to the middle of my high-topped shoes, I asked Annie to button the back of my white organdy apron. I watched, with envy, as my older sisters put on their grown-up capes and aprons. Mine was still a child's apron. Even Annie, only twelve, was allowed to wear an outfit like Mother's. The only part I didn't look forward to were those straight pins. I watched as Annie struggled with her cape, trying to cross it at the front just right and getting the pins in all the important places. No adults were permitted to use buttons or snaps on any of their garment, except underwear. Straight pins are used to close the front of the dress, fasten the apron at the side, and secure the cape to the apron.

After Annie had accomplished all this, it was time for her covering. The Amish believe that the hair needs to be covered at all times, even at night when sleeping. The covering is white organdy for Sunday, pleated by hand with small, intricate pleats. The Amish women pride themselves in their abilities to do neat and precise work. In fact, even though they aren't given too much latitude, the women are able to make their family's coverings unique and just a bit different from another family's caps (pronounced *"kops"*). The covering is then tied under the chin; it would be quite shameful if the wind blew it off and exposed the head full of braids. Even how much hair was allowed to show in front of the covering was regulated by the bishop of the individual congregations. We were allowed to show one inch, no more. If more hair was visible, according to our teachings, we were taught that that woman was worldly.

I was the first one ready that day and had time to take a peek out of the upstairs window. What a sight! This was the only kind of parade I had ever seen and I never tired of it. Our long lane was lined with the color black. Buggy after buggy crawled slowly, being pulled by

horses, which were well trained to be obedient and patient. My eyes traveled to the roads and from every direction I could see the black carriages coming to the Yoder farm. Some buggies carried only two . . . a grandma and a grandpa. Most looked lopsided as children had to be placed wherever possible. There were even two-seated buggies holding the big families of ten to thirteen children. Some families had to bring two buggies.

On this particular day, I had the opportunity to announce to the family the beginning of OUR DAY.

"Sie Kuma, Sie Kuma, Sie Kuma," (they come) I yelled as I clomped down the steps two at a time, trying not to get tangled in my long dress.

THE CHURCH SERVICE

"O Gott Fater, Wir Loben Dich." They were singing the second song, the prayer song, and still a few people were coming in. The latecomers were always the ones with many small children. It was hard to get a family of 12 or 13 ready and still be on time for the nine o'clock services.

Although most German songs that the Amish sing are only four or five verses long, it takes almost a half hour to sing one song because of the slow and mournful way they're done. There are no notes in an Amish hymnal, therefore tunes are all handed down through the generations by memory. Most Sunday mornings, they sang three songs.

When church service was held at our house and I was allowed to stay in the washhouse to watch the milk in the kettle, I enjoyed the singing most. It sounded so beautiful, standing apart and listening to it, rather than participating.

I was stirring the milk that special day when my friend Naomi came into the washhouse to say hello to me. They weren't even finished singing and already Naomi was allowed to go to the outhouse. OUR mother never let us make that trip until the sermon was well under way. Even then, she didn't always let us go, especially if she remembered that we went two weeks ago at the last church service. I never could figure out what going one week had to do with going two weeks later, but Mother felt her thinking was valid.

Naomi was often permitted to do things that we weren't. I remember her telling me in school that her parents even let her go sledding with their "English" neighbors. Anyone who is not Amish is called "English."

"Did you see Mahlon's new baby?" Naomi asked me. "This is the first Sunday they brought him."

"He sure cries a lot," I told Naomi. "I heard him clear out here. Maybe he needs *bletched* already."

"Oh, I don't think so," Wise Naomi said. "He probably just has a bellyache. You know a baby should not be paddled until he's a couple of months old. Well, I'd better do my business and get back inside before Mom comes looking for me," she whispered as she left.

She lifted her skirt just a little as she went up the one step out of the washhouse and, just as she had intended, I noticed her new shoes. It was a wonder she didn't brag to me about them. Why, it was only days ago that she had told me she had a hole in the bottom of her sole and already she had new shoes. They sure must have more money than our family has . . . I wouldn't have been allowed to get a new pair that soon.

Annie had been right when she told me the day before that someone might bring their child into the washhouse to *bletch* and that's why we had to clean it. The first sermon had barely started when Jonas Mandy brought both Levi and Katie out. She took them behind the washing machine and gave them both several swats and then told them not to cry.

On the way out, she turned to me and said, *"Wie alt bist du now?"*

That's the only question anyone ever asked me. How old are you? After I answered that I was eight, she said, "Pretty big for your age, huh?" She meant it as a compliment, but I didn't like it. I couldn't help that I was a little fat. I had to eat what we had. It probably was the *rivvel soup* or maybe the *schnitz pies* and I liked them both. Just thinking about the *schnitz pies* made me hungry. I could just see the trays of half-moon, apple-filled goodies in our pantry right now, waiting to be eaten by the hungry worshippers. I wondered if Mom would see me if I tried to sneak into the pantry and get one. I'd even settle for a sugar or molasses cookie. I decided to keep stirring the milk. I sure didn't need a *bletching* today.

Annie came into the washhouse just then, carrying our sister, Fannie.

"They're giving *zeigness* now (meaning the service was almost over). She handed me a dripping wet baby. "Mom said that you're supposed to take care of Fannie and change her diaper."

I would rather have listened to *zeigness.* I liked hearing the older, respected men in the congregation give witness that what they heard that morning was the truth. My grandfather had been one of these men . . . he often gave *zeigness.*

I heard the shuffling and knew the church was out. Now, the men would go outside and smoke and the women would rearrange the rooms with tables for the meal. As soon as the tables were set with kettles of bean soup, *schnitz pies* and cookies, bread and applebutter, pickles and red beets, the men came back in to eat. They ate at one table, the older women at another and the teenagers in the basement. Women with small children fed them in a corner of the kitchen. After the meal, everyone visited for the afternoon, allowing themselves enough time to get home in time to do the chores.

This exact same pattern would be repeated in two weeks at someone else's house. To deviate from the ritual handed down from their forefathers is considered the greatest sin of all.

Watching the buggies pull out that evening was kind of sad. It meant OUR DAY was over. We had worked hard for this special day and now it was over. We would not have church at our house again for another year.

I wondered if my teenaged sisters had asked Mom and Dad for permission to have singing that night. I sure hoped so. Although I wasn't

allowed to participate, nothing could stop me from hearing.

Whoever had the church service could decide whether they wanted to let the young people have singing at their house or not that evening. Word would spread quickly . . . whatever the decision. These singings were actually occasions for dating. Although they did sing, flirting was really the reason to have these gatherings. Weddings and threshings were other occasions for teenagers to get together and match up.

Annie came out to the grape arbor where I was standing, watching the buggies leave, and told me that there would be singing at our place that night. Even though I would be sent to bed, I would still be able to hear the singing downstairs. What a beautiful way to end OUR DAY.

OUR OWN *"SCHNUCK BUPLY"*

"Barbara, you take Fannie's hand and I'll bring Lizzie," sister Annie said that warm fall day. "We're going to Tobe's for awhile, maybe even overnight."

As soon as she said that "maybe overnight" I knew what was going on. *Somehow* another baby was going to come into our home. I had no idea where these babies came from, but the only time we ever stayed overnight at anyone's house, it was at our nearest Amish neighbor, and then only when a new addition was added to our family.

As the four of us walked out the lane I wondered why we could not have stayed home. I really wanted to find out where the next baby came from. Annie said the doctor came sometimes so I figured he must bring it. I just could not understand how he knew to bring an Amish baby . . . and then *if* he did bring it, why was Mom sick for awhile? It sure did not make sense.

When we arrived at the neighbor's house Annie said to the kindly old gentleman and his wife, "Mom said we should stay here until Dad comes and gets us." I watched them both smile. They knew something too and I was sure *they* wouldn't tell me anymore than my parents did. I knew better than to ask

questions. The only one I ever asked questions to was my sister and she didn't know much more about babies than I did.

After supper, I watched as our hosts put blankets on the floor and I knew we were not going home. Fannie was fussy all night so we didn't get much sleep. She was only two years old and I'm sure she missed Mom even more than the rest of us did.

After breakfast the next morning, the door opened and there stood our Dad.

"I've come to take the children home. They have a new baby sister," he said to our kind neighbors who had cared for us overnight. "Thanks for watching them. I hope you won't have to do it too many more times."

Although I watched the adults exchange smiles, I didn't understand what my Dad meant by that last statement.

That made number ten . . . 3 boys and 7 girls. They named her Katie. The Amish name their first four children after the two sets of grandparents and the rest after the aunts and uncles on both sides of the family. There are only about 20 names that the Amish use for the first names and there are also only about 20 last names.

First names for girls are usually Cora, Mattie, Annie, Lizzie, Barbara, Fannie, Katie, Mary, Naomi, Emma, Jemima, Ella, Sarah, Levina and Mandy.

First names for boys are John, Mose,

Ferdinand, Dannie, Sam, Amos, Albert, Emanual, Levi, Rudy, Enos, Eli, Jacob and Joseph.

Some of the last names are Yoder, Miller, Troyer, Byler, Hostetler, Hershberger, Stoltzfus, Detweiler, Schwartzentruber, Raber, Keim and Stutzman.

When we arrived at our house that morning, there lay our new sister, Katie, all dressed in Amish clothes. Sure enough, the doctor knew to bring another Amish baby. He sure was smart.

For several weeks our older sisters, Cora and Mattie, became our substitute mother while our Mom stayed in the bedroom.

When the older ones in the family were born, a young teenage cousin would come and be our "Maude" (hired girl). She stayed for a number of weeks, taking care of the house and babies while our mother recuperated.

The morning after Katie was born, I told Naomi on the way to school that I thought it was kinda dumb that Mom had to go to bed when the doctor did all the work.

THE MOVE

Although my brother Danny was almost eighteen years old, the steering wheel of a car was completely foreign to him. Until then the reins of a horse, hitched to a buggy, had been his "steering wheel." Being the oldest son in an Amish family, he was given many responsibilities early in his life. Driving a horse and buggy was something he started doing before he went to first grade.

Now, it was moving day and not only was our family leaving the Amish community, we were leaving the religion behind as well. We had traded our horse and buggy for a car . . . the ultimate symbol of leaving the Amish religion.

My parents had heard there was a Mennonite settlement in the next county, and were now moving their ten children to this more progressive community.

Brother Danny was given the job of transporting seven of his brothers and sisters to their new home eighty miles north. Mom, Dad and babies rode in the big truck that was hauling our belongings to our new address.

Even though I had to share the small back seat of our newly acquired automobile with four sisters, I didn't complain about being

squished. I was too excited. Actually, I was both excited and nervous and even a bit sad. Sister Annie and I turned around and peeked out the back window of the car as we neared the end of the lane. Annie had tears in her eyes watching our old house disappear into the landscape.

"Do you think we'll ever come back?" I whispered to Annie, trying to hide my excitement at the anticipation of what lay ahead in our new life. I was looking forward to seeing all the things I had been admiring for years in our mail-order catalog.

She didn't answer me. I guess she didn't feel much like talking. My older sisters were not talking either and neither was my brother Danny. He was concentrating on driving. He didn't want to get picked up by the police. After all, Dad never did find time to take him for his driver's license. Out of desperation I started talking to brother Ferdinand. He always liked to talk, but I usually only talked to him when I was bored. HE always had a way of making me mad. Like calling me dumb names. One name he always called me was Jerse . . . short for Jersey cow. I guess he did that because I was always a little chubby. But that wasn't my fault. It was the fattening food the Amish cook and eat. Just thinking about the mashed potatoes we ate at most meals made me hungry. These were not just regular old mashed potatoes. The Amish, after piling a bowl full of the fluffy white starch, make little dents in the mound with the back

of a spoon. Into these cavities they pour melted, browned butter.

One time Ferdinand very seriously challenged me to a roasting-ear eating contest. I ate one dozen ears of corn and he kept going. But he had what he needed. From then on he would say to anyone who would listen, "Do you know Jerse can eat a dozen ears of corn at one time?" I just about hated him then. But with our Amish teaching, we were not allowed to hate. I sure was glad we were leaving the Amish.

Ferdinand and I read road signs the entire eighty miles to our new home. I was proud of the fact that *I* could pronounce more words than he could, even though he was a year older than I was. The only road signs we were accustomed to reading was "County Road 94" that we passed as we walked to and from our one-room country school. We rarely went to town, so we enjoyed our glimpse of the outside world as we traveled on the highways that memorable day.

I was in the fifth grade and just knew I'd be as smart as anyone in the new school we would be attending. But I was quickly deflated as I spotted a sign that day that read, "Fire Dept." I didn't know what a "Dept." was.

We pulled into the lane of the house our parents had picked out several months before. This was the first time we children had seen it. Although I really was not expecting it to look like an Amish house, it was hard to switch my mind from all the houses I was used to. Before us stood a modern looking house (actually it was an old farm house). What made it look modern were the telephone and electricity wires that were connected to it. I could hardly wait to try out these new contraptions. No more kerosine lamps. I was not sure why we would need the telephone, although I suspected it would come in handy sometime if Mom would have another baby. She would need a doctor or someone to help her. When we were Amish, Dad always went after help with the horse and buggy when Mom's time came, but often did not get back in time.

Of course, brother Ferdinand was the first one in the door of our new house. He always had to be first. I was second. He found the light switches and I found the window blinds. We worked them awhile and then we traded off. What a joy. What delightful toys. Soon our younger brothers and sisters joined us in our fun.

We could tell by the sound of rushing water that a new plaything was discovered on the second floor. We all rushed upstairs to see for ourselves what all the commotion was about. We were a bit disappointed because we had to wait for the tank to refill before the next one could take a turn flushing this fascinating invention.

Our new house was full of new and strange things. In the kitchen was a stove that did not need coal and wood. There was an icebox that did not need ice. The floor had linoleum, not bare wood. There were built-in cupboards with counter tops. Water ran from pipes into a sink without the aid of a handpump.

In the basement was a washing machine that had a motor to run it. An enormous furnace stood in the cellar that would heat the *entire* house. No more huddling around a small stove in the living room and no more cold bedrooms with ice on the *inside* of the window sill.

I could tell our life was going to be much easier.

Although it was fascinating and exciting to discover these fancy gadgets, the mood that day was not entirely happy. The older ones in the family were experiencing traumatic feelings, leaving behind their close friends. They would try to keep in touch with letters, but they knew, deep in their hearts, that things would never be the same.

We had crossed the bridge.

Recipes

SOME FOOD WE ATE WHILE I WAS AMISH

Bean Soup

Rivvel Soup

Banana Soup

Strawberry Soup

Raspberry Soup

Sugar Cookies

Molasses Cookies

Schnitz Pies

Bread

Knepp

Pudding (Banana, Graham Cracker)

Apple Cream Pie

Mom

6 A.M.

7 A.M.

10 A.M.

HOMEMADE BREAD

Pour 4 cups of warm water over 3 tblsp. or 3 paks of yeast. Add 2 tblsp. salt and ½ cup sugar. Let stand a few minutes to foam.

Work in approx. 10 cups flour and several tblsp. oil or melted shortening.

Let raise, punch down and let raise again.

Put into pans, poke holes in dough with fork and let raise in pans. Bake at 375 degrees for 20-25 min. for 1 lb. loaves, longer for larger loaves. Makes 5 - 1 lb. loaves.

For wheat or rye bread, use 6 cups white flour and 4 cups wheat or rye flour.

SCHNITZ PIES

Use a good pie crust recipe and roll approximately 8" in diameter. Filling is a mixture of applesauce and apple butter (mix to taste). Spread filling on one-half of crust, fold in half and flute tightly so mixture does not leak. These will be half-moon pies. The Amish make these with dried apples but the same taste can be achieved by using the applesauce and applebutter mixture. Bake in moderate oven.

BEAN SOUP (served at church service)

Melt butter, size of walnut) in heavy pan and put in pre-cooked soup beans (2 cups). After beans are heated, fill pan almost full with milk (approx. 1½ qts.). Heat to boiling point and just before serving, add chunks of bread. Be careful not to put too much bread in the soup or it will be too thick. Salt and pepper to taste.

RIVVEL SOUP

In heavy pan slowly heat 2 qts. of milk. While milk is heating, beat one egg with a fork and add enough flour to make crumbs. Sprinkle crumbs into hot milk. Salt and pepper to taste.

FRUIT SOUP

We ate a lot of fruit soup . . . whatever was in season. Favorites were strawberries and raspberries. Banana Soup is made this way, too. Mash fruit, add sugar and plenty of milk. Add bread chunks.

PEANUT BUTTER - SYRUP SPREAD

The Amish mix dark Karo syrup with peanut butter to make a spread for bread.

Desserts

Our desserts were fruit pies and a few cookies listed here, and puddings.

Banana Pudding is simply layers of corn starch pudding - graham cracker crumbs mixed with sugar and bananas.

These puddings were generally served for company dinners in glass bowls with a stem.

DATE NUT PUDDING WITH CARMEL SAUCE

1 cup boiling water
1 cup dates
Pour water of dates - set aside to cool.
Then add remaining ingredients.
1 cup sugar
1½ cups flour
½ cup chopped nuts
1 tsp. butter
1 tsp. vanilla
1 egg
1 tsp. soda
Pnch salt
Bake in a cake pan - when cold, break up in pieces and fold into caramel sauce. Just before serving top with whipped cream.

CARAMEL SAUCE

2 cups brown sugar
½ cup cream
½ cup butter
Pinch soda
Mix butter and soda with brown sugar and cream. Cook until it candies. Cool before folding date pudding into it.

APPLE CREAM PIE

Into unbaked pie shell put small handful of flour and large handful of white sugar. Arrange apple slices neatly in a single layer. Fill the crust with a rich cream or evaporated milk. Sprnkle top with small handful of brown sugar, dot with butter and sprinkle with cinnamon. Bake in a moderate oven.

CANE MOLASSES COOKIES

2 cups cane molasses
1 cup white sugar
1 cup lard
3 eggs
3 tsp. soda
Vanilla
2 tsp. ginger (or any spice preferred)
Flour - enough to make a stiff batter
Roll and cut with cookie cutter. They will not turn out right if dropped.
Put together in order listed.

GINGER COOKIES

2 cups brown sugar
1½ cups shortening
2 eggs
½ cup maple syrup or molasses
4 tsp. soda
2 tsp. cinnamon
1 tsp. cloves
2 tsp. ginger
½ tsp. salt
4½ cups flour
Mix well and form into walnut size balls. Roll in sugar and bake 5 - 8 minutes at 350 degrees.

KNEPP

1 cup flour
2 tsp. baking powder
Stir in milk to thick - drop into bubbling mixture.
Good in elderberry juice, fruits of any kind or even in meat broths.

SUGAR COOKIES

1 cup white sugar
2 cups brown sugar
1¼ cups shortening
4 eggs
1¼ cups cream or evaporated milk
1 tsp. vanilla
2 tsp. baking powder
Flour - to make not too stiff dough (approx. 5 cups)
Pinch salt

When rolling out - sprinkle white sugar over top and roll sugar in very lightly. Bake about 10 minutes at 350 degrees. This makes about 5½ dozen cookies about 4" in diameter.

MAIL ORDER BLANK

Please send ______ copies of "Born Amish" to the address below.

Name ______________________________

Address ______________________________

City ______________ State __________ Zip ________

Enclosed is $ ____________ (Check or money order - Do NOT send cash). Send $5.95 ($4.95 for book plus $1.00 shipping and handling) for each book ordered. OHIO RESIDENTS ADD 25c PER BOOK SALES TAX. Foreign orders $6.95 ($5.95 for book plus $2.00 shipping and handling) for each book ordered. Allow 4 to 6 weeks for delivery.

SEND ORDERS TO: JACBAR PUBLICATIONS - Box 103 - Randolph, Ohio 44265